BE
STRONG

BE STRONG

An Hachette UK Company
www.hachette.co.uk

Vie Books, an imprint of Summersdale Publishers Ltd
Part of Octopus Publishing Group Limited
Carmelite House
50 Victoria Embankment
LONDON
EC4Y 0DZ
UK

www.summersdale.com

Printed and bound in China

ISBN: 978-1-78783-607-5

Substantial discounts on bulk quantities of Summersdale books are available to corporations, professional associations and other organizations. For details contact general enquiries: telephone: +44 (0) 1243 771107 or email: enquiries@summersdale.com.

BE
STRONG

You Are Braver Than You Think

Poppy O'Neill

CONTENTS

PART 3: CONFIDENCE BUILDERS 54

PART 4: LOOKING AFTER YOURSELF 96

FOREWORD

Amanda Ashman-Wymbs, Counsellor and Psychotherapist, registered and accredited by the British Association for Counselling and Psychotherapy

Having worked therapeutically with children and adolescents in school and in the private sector for over a decade, and through raising two daughters of my own, it is clear that issues of confidence can cause a lot of suffering and many problems for children today.

Our current culture often puts children under a lot of pressure in different ways, with the result being that they can end up feeling very unsure of themselves and their abilities.

They can lose sight of their natural confidence, often needing some help to find their inner strength again and relearn how to deal with the internal and external challenges they face, in a confident and relaxed way.

Poppy O'Neill's workbook *Be Strong* is a great supportive resource for both parents and children. It helps the child understand what confidence is, what may affect it and clarifies that levels of confidence are something that can and will fluctuate in relation to circumstance.

The book is empathetic in its style, and works to build resilience and self-knowledge in the child. It gives practical guidance and clear examples in taking steps to build confidence, covers the difference between assertiveness, passivity and aggression, and helps the child to know what the qualities of a true friendship are. The book also teaches the child how to use active imagination in the form of affirmations and visualizations to support confidence, build new habits and find solutions.

I highly recommend this self-help book for children. It's a truly great resource filled with fun activities that will help children to learn skills and gain knowledge and insights that will support them in being more confident for the rest of their lives.

INTRODUCTION: A GUIDE FOR PARENTS AND CARERS

Be Strong is a practical guide to self-confidence for children. Using activities and ideas based on therapeutic techniques developed by child psychologists, this book will help your child build their self-confidence and think differently about how their thoughts and emotions affect the way they see the world.

Confidence is the ability to take action in the face of uncertainty. As a child's self-awareness and knowledge of the world grows, they get a sense of how it feels to be embarrassed, hurt or to fail and their confidence can take a dive.

We all struggle with confidence sometimes – and everyone has their insecurities – but your child might seem more prone to self-doubt than others their age. Sometimes, no matter how much you reassure them, certain things can prey on their minds. The thing about confidence is, it's a lot more about *acting* confident… feeling confident comes later on, with experience.

This book is aimed at children aged 7–11, an age where a lot of things change. School gets more serious, friendships can become more complex, their bodies start to change, and often children start to take a greater interest in their physical appearance and that of others at this stage. With all these new and somewhat daunting experiences, it's no wonder some children lack the confidence to cope with these things head-on. If this sounds like your child, you're far from alone. With your support and gentle encouragement in the right direction, it's possible to build up their self-confidence and help them navigate challenges, feel happier in themselves and grow into a strong, independent young person.

Signs of low confidence in children

Look out for signs such as these as they can help you determine if your child is suffering with low self-confidence:

- They are reluctant to try new things

- They find small changes very difficult

- They are overly concerned with fitting in with their peers

- They are easily stressed at the prospect of potential failure

- They experience mood swings

Keep a diary to help you get a better understanding of how often your child experiences low self-confidence, or if it's a constant problem. It's also helpful to note what else is going on in your child's life, as it's not always immediately obvious where their behaviour stems from and what triggers a dip in confidence.

It's important to remember that taking an interest in your child's emotional health is a difficult step but an incredibly positive one. It's OK if you're unsure how to help your child or what to do. Self-confidence is a lifelong habit rather than something that can be achieved quickly and simply – meaning it's never too late to start building it.

Starting the conversation with your child

Confidence is complex and unique for everyone and it's hard to talk about in specific terms. The best way to talk to your child is simply to open a conversation about their day and see where it goes. If you sense a lack of confidence about something, gently ask questions about that aspect of your child's life.

In order to grow in confidence, your child will need to do some things that they find scary. So, when they talk about the things they find difficult, it's really important to validate how they feel.

It can be tempting to minimize their worries by saying "you'll be fine" or "that won't happen". But while it can feel like the best and kindest thing to do, this approach can mean that children start to feel ashamed of their fears and insecurities, making them even harder to address.

Instead, listen to your child and validate their feelings. You can use phrases like "that sounds really scary/upsetting/difficult" to let them know their feelings are understandable and that they make sense.

Confidence comes when we know that we will be OK if we feel upsetting emotions. Let your child know that, whatever happens, you love them and they will cope.

How to use this book

This book is for your child, so the level of input you have will depend on how much they want or need. Some children might be happy working through the activities under their own steam, while others might need a little guidance and encouragement.

Let your child know it's OK to go at their own pace and let them do so independently. Growing confidence means trusting in their abilities and allowing them to make their own decisions.

The activities are designed to get your child thinking about themselves and the way their mind works, helping them to act with bravery and grow their self-confidence.

Hopefully this book with be helpful for you and your child, enabling greater understanding of how confidence works and how to build it. However, if you have any serious concerns about your child's mental health, your GP is the best person to go to for further advice.

HOW TO USE THIS BOOK: A GUIDE FOR CHILDREN

These are signs that you may have low confidence:

- ♥ Feel scared to try new things

- ♥ Find it hard to speak up

- ♥ Want to change yourself in order to fit in with your friends

- ♥ Feel like you aren't good enough compared to others

- ♥ Think that things will always go wrong for you

If that sounds like you sometimes, or all of the time, this book is here to help. You have the power to change how you see yourself, and the bravery to do things that are difficult.

Inside this book you'll find information and ideas on how confidence works and how you can build yours, as well as activities to help you understand yourself and boost self-confidence.

You can read the book at your own pace – there's no need to rush. There might be things in here that you want to talk about with a trusted adult. That could be your mum or dad, your carer, one of your teachers, an older brother or sister, grandparent, aunt, uncle, neighbour, or any other adult that you know well and feel comfortable talking to.

This book is for you and about you, so you're the expert and there are no wrong answers!

INTRODUCING PIP THE MONSTER

Hello! I'm Pip and I'm here to guide you through this book. There are a lot of fun activities to try and interesting ideas to think about. Are you ready? Let's go!

PART 1: WHAT IS CONFIDENCE?

What does it mean?

When we talk about confidence, what do we mean? Some people might think confidence means being loud or putting your ideas first over other people's, but that's not quite right.

Confidence comes from feeling sure of yourself and your abilities. When you believe in yourself, you know you can try new things and speak your mind. When someone is confident, they don't let worries about making a mistake or disagreeing with someone else stop them.

Confident people don't get their confidence from making fun of others. If someone does that, it means they are lacking in confidence and are making the mistake of thinking they will feel good by making others feel bad.

Feelings of confidence can go up and down depending on how you're feeling and what's happening around you. There are a lot of things you can do to help increase your confidence levels, and this book is designed to help you find the best ones for you.

ACTIVITY: ALL ABOUT ME!

First things first. Let's find out more about you and what matters to you. Doodle your answers in the frames.

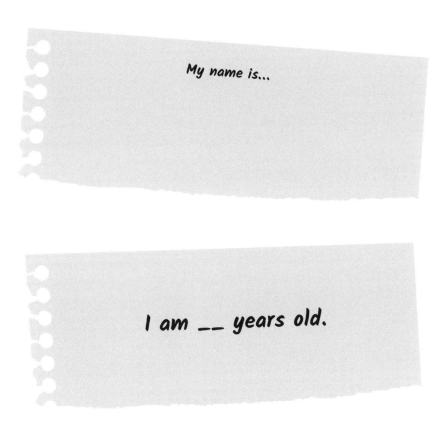

My name is...

I am __ years old.

My family members are...

Three words that describe where I live...

My favourite things are...

ACTIVITY: WHAT MAKES ME SPECIAL

The most special and unique thing about every human being is how we think and feel... our inner world! Can you complete these sentences?

I'm good at _____.

I worry about _____.

I'm proud of _____.

I dream about _____.

I used to _____.

I always _____.

I never _____.

I'm interested in _____.

_____ makes me laugh.

_____ makes me sad.

_____ makes me angry.

I AM WONDERFUL EXACTLY AS I AM

ACTIVITY: MAKE A MANDALA

A mandala is a circular pattern, usually but not always symmetrical, like the one below (you can colour it in, if you like).

You can make your own mandala out of almost anything – pebbles, leaves, books, flower petals, Lego bricks, buttons… or a mix of these! All you need to do is arrange them in a circular pattern.

Try making your own – being creative just for fun is a great way to build confidence.

Signs of low and high self-confidence

Having low self-confidence feels like this:

- Feeling anxious often

- Feeling stuck or frozen with fear

- Believing that you are not as good as others

- Believing bad things will happen to you

- Disliking yourself

- Feeling ashamed of who you are or how you look

- Dreading everyday activities

- Lying or keeping quiet about your opinion in order to fit in

- Believing that you will fail if you try new things

- Feeling very afraid of making mistakes

Having high self-confidence feels like this:

- ♥ Feeling calm most of the time

- ♥ Feeling safe

- ♥ Enjoying your life

- ♥ Feeling OK with change

- ♥ Being able to talk about your feelings

- ♥ Being able to disagree with others

- ♥ Liking yourself

- ♥ Accepting who you are and how you look

- ♥ Feeling able to try new things

- ♥ Respecting other people and yourself

- ♥ Accepting that you will make mistakes and can learn from them

ACTIVITY: HOW CONFIDENT DO YOU FEEL RIGHT NOW?

Can you rate your confidence right at this moment? You might like to think about how confident you feel about reading this book, or something that you'll be doing later today or tomorrow. Jot down some notes so you remember the reasons and feelings!

0   1   2   3   4   5   6   7   8   9   10

Not at all confident   **Super confident**

_____

_____

_____

Come back to this activity another time, perhaps when you're feeling really confident:

0   1   2   3   4   5   6   7   8   9   10

Not at all confident   *Super confident*

_____

_____

_____

… and once more when you're feeling quite down about something:

0   1   2   3   4   5   6   7   8   9   10

Not at all confident   *Super confident*

_____

_____

_____

What is "self-talk"?

"Self-talk" means how we speak to and about ourselves. You might be thinking, "Don't be silly – I don't talk to myself!" but our thoughts have a voice, and how kindly or unkindly this voice speaks will make a big difference to your confidence levels.

Think of a time you made a mistake. Can you remember any of the words you used to talk about and to yourself, out loud or in your head? If so, can you write them below?

For example, "I always get it wrong" or "I'll try harder next time."

_____

_____

What you just wrote is an example of self-talk. How kind is your self-talk? Would you want to be friends with someone who spoke to you in that way?

If the answer is no, here's some good news: you can choose to speak to yourself more kindly. Every time you hear yourself thinking or saying something unkind about yourself, pick a kinder sentence.

For example:

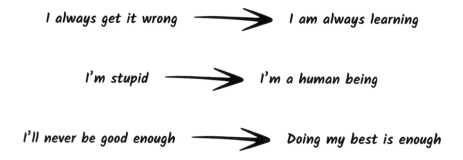

I always get it wrong ⟶ I am always learning

I'm stupid ⟶ I'm a human being

I'll never be good enough ⟶ Doing my best is enough

ACTIVITY: TELL A NEW STORY

In our heads, we're telling ourselves stories all day long! Sometimes we tell ourselves kind stories, and sometimes they're unkind.

Pip tripped over a log on the way to school one day.

In Pip's head the story went:

"I'm so stupid and everyone will laugh at me."

Can you think of a different, kinder story?

How about:

"I feel embarrassed! I didn't see that log. It could have happened to anyone."

One of Pip's friends saw Pip trip over and is smiling. Can you think of a kind story Pip's mind could tell?

_____

_____

_____

_____

Continue your story over the page

_____

_____

_____

_____

_____

_____

_____

_____

One of the best ways to grow more confident is to remember that every thought we have is a story. We can choose to tell ourselves kind stories or unkind ones – but just because we can choose, doesn't mean it's easy! Next time you're feeling low on confidence, try listening to the story in your mind, and choosing one that's a little bit kinder.

I AM LOVED

PART 2: CONFIDENCE BOOSTERS AND SHRINKERS

Confidence goes up and down for everyone – if some people don't ever seem low in confidence, they're probably just very good at pretending to be confident. That's not a bad thing. Pretending to be more confident than you really feel is often what it takes to act with confidence. Once you see that you can act that way and things turn out OK… or even turn out brilliantly… your confidence will grow. The key to being brave and acting like a confident person is taking the first step – even if it feels scary.

There are lots of things that might help you act with more confidence, and other things that will make you feel less confident. In this chapter we'll explore both!

ACTIVITY: WHAT HAPPENS WHEN IT'S TIME TO BE BRAVE?

Pip has decided to join a new sports club. It's Pip's first time and it takes a lot of bravery to find the confidence to try something new. What might be going on in Pip's mind? Let's take a look:

Can you think about what happens in your mind when it's time to do something brave? What kind of thoughts do you have?

We've looked at what happens in the mind when it's time to be brave. Now let's think about how it feels in your body. Here's how Pip's body feels:

Tummy ache

Sweating

Rapid heartbeat

I can't move

Can you write or draw how your body feels when you're trying to find bravery?

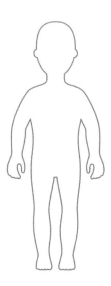

ACTIVITY: WHAT HAPPENS WHEN I'M FEELING BIG FEELINGS

When you're trying to find bravery and confidence, but you're feeling other big emotions, like fear or embarrassment, it can be really hard to think straight! Sometimes we start to panic and we do things to help us feel safe again, even if we're not really in danger.

What do you do when you feel big, overwhelming emotions? Circle the ones that sound like you – as many or as few as you like.

Hide myself

Put on a smile
and pretend
I'm OK

Get angry

Run away

Shout

Something else?

ACTIVITY: QUICK CONFIDENCE BOOSTERS

Here are a few ways to raise your confidence quickly. Do any of these work for you? You can add your own too!

- Kind words from others

- Kind words to yourself

- Wearing clothes you feel comfortable in

- Eating a healthy meal or snack

- A big gulp of water

- A hug

- Thinking of a time when things went well

- Playing with your friends

- _____

- _____

- _____

- _____

Listening to your body and mind

Confidence is a feeling inside your body together with a way of thinking about yourself. Sometimes the feeling might be small like a candle flame. Sometimes it might feel big like a bonfire. There will always be lots of feelings going on in your body – emotions and your organs working, as well as the things you can touch, smell, taste, see and hear.

Can you close your eyes and feel what is going on in your body right now? There's no need to name the feelings or write anything down – just listen to your body for a moment.

Now, can you do the same with your mind? Imagine sitting inside your own head and looking at thought bubbles. Again, there's no need to do anything – just watch and let your thoughts naturally come and go.

What is mindfulness?

When you quietly observe what you're thinking and feeling, it's called mindfulness. It's a bit like taking a little holiday from the rest of the world while you just hang out in your body for a moment. When you practise mindfulness, you get better at calming yourself down when you're feeling big or frightening emotions, which in turn helps you to act with confidence.

There are lots of different ways in which you can be mindful. On the next few pages there are some mindful activities to try – see which feel best for you!

ACTIVITY: HOW DO YOU FEEL RIGHT NOW?

Close your eyes and do a scan of your body – how does it feel on the top of your head? Move your attention slowly down until you get to your toes. Some parts might feel heavy or light, comfortable or uncomfortable, and you might be feeling emotions like worry or sensations in your body like hunger.

Can you decorate this picture to show how the different parts of your body feel? You can use colour, pattern, words, symbols… anything you can imagine.

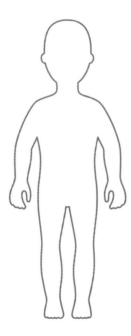

You can check in with your body any time – there's always something to feel!

ACTIVITY: 5-4-3-2-1 SENSES

You can do this activity any time, anywhere. Think about the things going on around you. Can you spot:

5 things you can see

_____

4 things you can feel

_____

3 things you can hear

_____

2 things you can smell

_____

1 thing you can taste

_____

♥ **If you have trouble with any of these, you can list your favourite things to see, feel, hear, smell or taste instead.**

ACTIVITY: GLITTER JAR

When you feel upset, panicked or worried, it can feel like you're all shaken up inside. A glitter jar can be a great tool to help you calm down.

You will need:

- A jar with a tight-fitting lid

- Water

- Biodegradable glitter in your favourite colour

Instructions:

1. Ask a grown-up to help you put the glitter in the jar. Then, fill it with water and screw the lid on securely (you could add a layer of waterproof tape to be extra safe).
2. Shake up the jar and watch the glitter go wild in the water. Now, hold the jar still or put it on a table. See how the glitter slowly and gently floats to the bottom of the jar.
3. Next time you're feeling shaken up inside, try shaking your glitter jar and imagining your feelings gently calming down at the same time as the glitter.

I CAN ASK
FOR WHAT
I NEED

ACTIVITY: MOOD TRACKER

Can you keep track of your mood for a week, a month, a year? First, give each emotion a colour and add more!

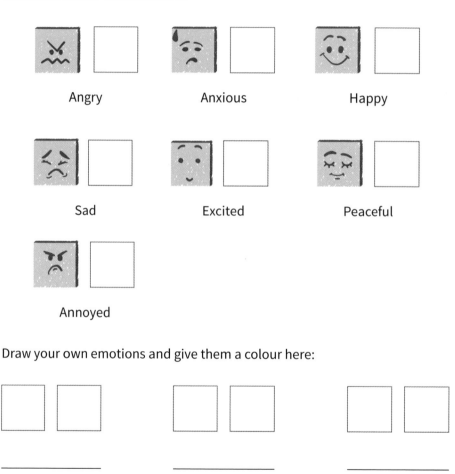

Angry   Anxious   Happy

Sad   Excited   Peaceful

Annoyed

Draw your own emotions and give them a colour here:

Now track your mood every day by colouring in the little squares on the facing page.

PART 2: CONFIDENCE BOOSTERS AND SHRINKERS

	Jan	Feb	Mar	Apr	May	Jun	Jul	Aug	Sep	Oct	Nov	Dec
1												
2												
3												
4												
5												
6												
7												
8												
9												
10												
11												
12												
13												
14												
15												
16												
17												
18												
19												
20												
21												
22												
23												
24												
25												
26												
27												
28												
29												
30												
31												

ACTIVITY: DRAW YOUR EMOTIONS

What are the emotions you feel most regularly? Can you draw them in these circles? You can use colour, texture, patterns, words… Don't be afraid to get really creative!

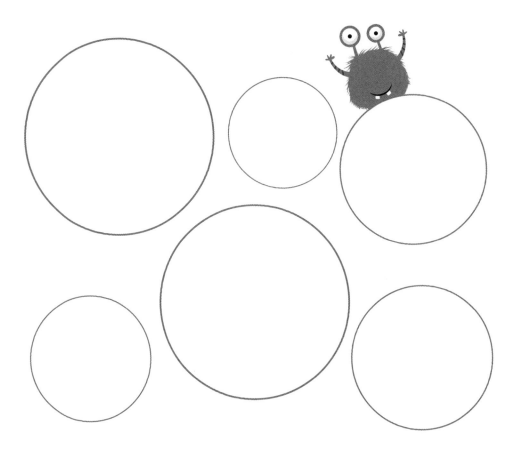

ACTIVITY: I CAN EXPRESS MY EMOTIONS!

How does it feel to let someone know the emotions you feel inside? It can sometimes take a lot of bravery and confidence to do this.

Emojis are a great way to start showing others how we feel inside.

How are these emojis feeling? What makes you feel that way too?

I feel _____

_____

_____

when _____

_____

_____

I feel _____

_____

_____

when _____

_____

_____

I feel _____

_____

_____

when _____

_____

_____

I feel _____   I feel _____   I feel _____

_____   _____   _____

_____   _____   _____

when _____   when _____   when _____

_____   _____   _____

_____   _____   _____

I LIKE MYSELF!

ACTIVITY: BE BODY CONFIDENT

Your body is amazing. It's just right for you – whatever shapes, sizes and colours make up your body. What's more, your body is working all the time – your brain is learning new things, your digestive system is taking the goodness from your food and getting rid of anything your body doesn't need. Your senses are taking in information from the world and your heart is pumping blood to every part of you.

Everyone's body is different, and everyone's body is beautiful.

Can you draw a self-portrait? You could use a mirror or draw yourself from memory.

Breathing techniques

When you're feeling low on confidence, doing brave things can feel really scary. When we feel scared, anxious or worried, our breathing can get fast and shallow. A good way to feel calmer and braver is to take deep breaths. Deep breathing calms your whole body – slowing your heartbeat and stopping any racing thoughts.

Practise these breathing exercises so you can try them next time you feel panicked or stressed.

Belly breathing

Grab a cuddly toy and lie down on your bed, sofa or on the floor. Put the toy on your tummy. Can you make the toy go up and down slowly, by breathing deeply into your tummy? Count your breaths and keep going until you get to 12.

Triangle breathing

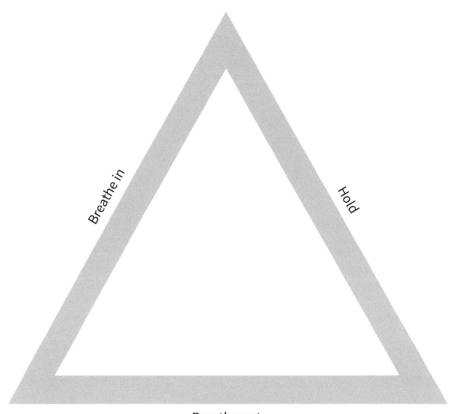

Breathe in

Hold

Breathe out

Trace your finger slowly along the edges of this triangle. Can you breathe in for the first side, hold your breath for the second, and breathe out as your finger travels along the third side? Keep going until you've been around the whole triangle five times.

ACTIVITY: ONE-MINUTE VISUALIZATION

When you're feeling low on confidence or worried about something that's going to take bravery, try visualization. All you need to do is sit quietly and think about these words. You could read the words, set a timer for one minute and visualize the imagery, or ask a grown-up to read the words to you.

Imagine you are a mighty tree. Feel how your roots reach deep into the ground, supporting you and bringing you everything you need to grow even more mighty. Feel how strong your trunk is, how still and sturdy. Feel your branches and how they reach upward, always growing. Feel your leaves – how does the warm sun feel on them? How about the cool rain? Sometimes the wind will rustle your leaves. Some might even be blown away. In the autumn, they all fall away. But you are always growing, and in the spring your branches are even taller, your new leaves even greener. Now feel slowly back down your branches – there's no rush. Feel through your trunk – notice how it's a little stronger now – and into the ground to your roots, which now stretch a little deeper. When you're ready, you can open your eyes.

❤ **Visualizing like this will help you feel calmer and more confident. Doing it regularly is a great way to build confidence. The best thing about visualization is, the more you do it, the more enjoyable it is!**

Sitting with tricky emotions

Acting with bravery and confidence can be really uncomfortable. It takes huge strength to feel afraid and carry on anyway. A very good way of building confidence is to get used to feeling emotions that are uncomfortable. A lot of the time, it feels good to push away tricky emotions like fear, by choosing not to act with bravery. If you do that, it's OK! No one is brave all the time – that would be exhausting. But when something is really worth it, like learning a fun new skill or making an interesting new friend, you can sit with uncomfortable emotions and do the brave thing.

So, just because it feels scary to talk to someone you'd like to get to know, it doesn't mean you shouldn't do it. And even though a new skill might be hard to learn and you may feel embarrassed, it doesn't mean you shouldn't do it. Most of the time, the greatest fun is just the other side of fear. Once you get through the fear, the fun will be there waiting for you.

I CAN TAKE
A DEEP BREATH

PART 3:
CONFIDENCE BUILDERS

Confidence is something that needs to be built, like a tower. Doing brave things is the best way to build your confidence. The braver you act, the braver you'll feel! In this chapter we'll look at ways to build strength and help you grow in confidence.

ACTIVITY: SMALL STEPS

When something feels enormous and you think you can't do it, it's time to break it down into small steps, like this.

Pip has a new bike and doesn't feel confident about riding it yet. Pip's friends whizz around the park on their bikes, and Pip worries about feeling embarrassed in front of them. Pip is still a bit wobbly on this new, bigger bike. How can Pip break down bike riding into small steps?

First, Pip finds a quiet place to practise. Without other children watching, Pip doesn't feel so worried about wobbly riding.

Next, Pip makes a plan to practise every day for a week.

On the first day, Pip wobbles and falls off the bike (of course, Pip's wearing a helmet and knee pads), but Pip doesn't give up!

Each day, Pip gets a little less wobbly and a little more confident.

When Pip feels ready, Pip picks a quiet time at the park, when there's no one else there. Pip rides around the park to see how it feels.

When it feels OK – but still a little bit scary – Pip finds enough bravery to ride with friends. It's a lot of fun and even though Pip's still a tiny bit wobbly, Pip feels confident about riding a bike at the park now.

Here are Pip's steps:

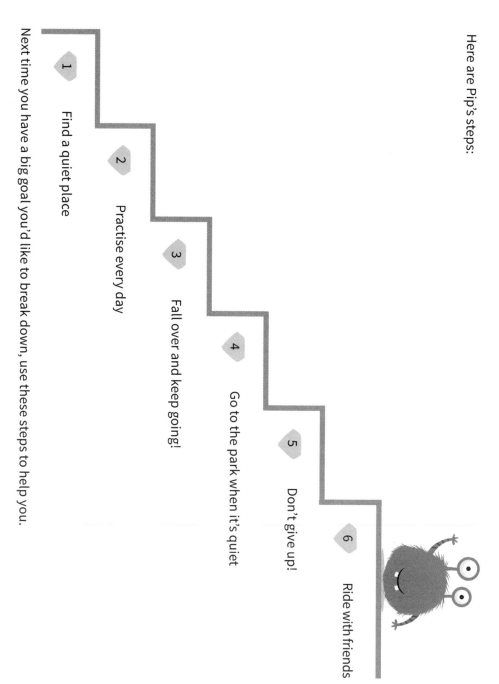

1 Find a quiet place

2 Practise every day

3 Fall over and keep going!

4 Go to the park when it's quiet

5 Don't give up!

6 Ride with friends

Next time you have a big goal you'd like to break down, use these steps to help you.

Feel braver!

As we've learned in this book so far, often you have to do things while you still feel a bit scared in order to grow your confidence. Here are some ideas to help you on your way to feeling braver and more confident:

- Sing along to a confident song (loudly)

- Hold a lucky stone, crystal or teddy

- Say an affirmation five times (see page 83)

- Hug someone special

- Stroke a pet

- Draw your feelings

- Write down your worries and rip them up

- Stretch

- Do some jumping jacks

- Shake your body

- Take three deep breaths

- Blow up a balloon

ACTIVITY: STAND TALL

When you need a confidence boost, try changing the way you hold your body. Pull your shoulders back and down, straighten your spine and raise your chin. These "power poses" will help you get in the zone – copy Pip and see how a different pose can change how you feel.

Y for yes

I'm in charge

Reach for the stars

Ta-da!

What is "assertiveness"?

Have you heard of "assertiveness"? When someone is confident, they act assertively. It means speaking up for yourself while also considering how other people might feel. It's like the middle of this see-saw:

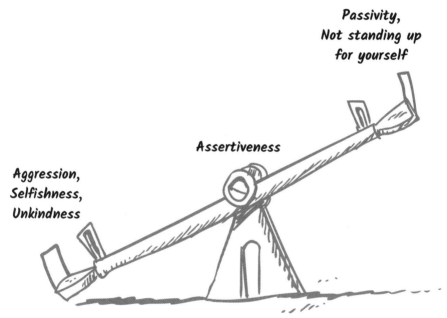

Being assertive can feel quite scary. Often it's easier to let others have their way and keep your own feelings a secret – that's called being passive. Or it might feel more comfy to scare the other person so you get your way – behaving in this way is called being aggressive.

The truth is, it's OK to speak your mind and ask for what you want. Other people might have different ideas or opinions, and that's OK too. When you speak and act assertively, you are clear about what you think and feel, and you respect what other people think and feel too.

Pip is enjoying reading a new book by a favourite author when Pip's friend starts playing a noisy computer game nearby.

How might Pip respond?

Can you work out which response is passive, which is aggressive and which is assertive? Draw a line between the response and your answer.

A	Ignore the noisy game	Assertive
B	Steal their control pad	Passive
C	Ask them to turn down the volume	Aggressive

When we act assertively, everyone feels important and respected.

Answer: A = passive, B = aggressive, C = assertive

ACTIVITY: TRY NEW THINGS TOOLBOX

Can you think of something that used to be difficult or scary for you and now feels easier?

_____

_____

_____

Can you remember what helped you to keep trying when it felt difficult?

_____

_____

_____

Trying new things and dealing with change can be really hard. Is there something you're struggling with right now?

_____

_____

_____

One thing that can help is doing a "rehearsal". You can act this out in real life, perhaps with a parent or carer who can play different parts. You can also do it in writing or by drawing.

Try writing about the things you're worried might happen:

_____

_____

_____

_____

_____

Now can you write about the best way it could turn out? How would you like to feel? What would you like to do? What would you like to happen?

_____

_____

_____

_____

_____

What makes a good/bad friend

How can you tell if someone is a good friend to you? It can be harder than it sounds, and school can sometimes feel like a competition to have the most friends – no matter if they're good ones or bad ones.

Just because someone spends time with you and calls themselves your friend doesn't mean they're a true friend. When you're with a true friend, you can relax and be yourself. With a false friend you might feel tense, worried and like you need to keep secrets about yourself.

When you're feeling low in confidence, it can be especially hard to say no to false friends. Having lots of friends can be a confidence booster, but that confidence only sticks around if they're true friends. A bad friend will bring your confidence right back down again.

Remember: you deserve friends who treat you well and you don't have to spend time around people who make you feel bad about yourself.

A true friend:

- ♥ Listens to you

- ♥ Talks to you kindly

- ♥ Stands up for you

- ♥ Includes you

- ♥ Celebrates your achievements

A false friend:

- ♥ Ignores you

- ♥ Talks to you unkindly

- ♥ Leaves you out

- ♥ Hurts your body and/or your feelings

- ♥ Teases or embarrasses you

- ♥ **If you're being bullied, it's not your fault and you don't deserve it. Bullying can be with words or actions and it's never OK. If you think you're being bullied, you can go to a trusted grown-up and ask for help.**

What kind of friend am I?

What are the things that your friends like about you? If that's a tricky question to answer, why not ask them?

Maybe your friends love your laugh, your listening skills or the way you tell a story…

Write or draw your answers below.

♥ Being yourself is always the best way to find good friends. If you hide your true self away, how will potential friends know how amazing you are?

I DESERVE TO BE TREATED WITH KINDNESS

ACTIVITY: PUT YOURSELF IN THEIR SHOES

When there's a problem or argument, how does that feel? Conflict can bring up big feelings in everyone.

If you take the time to put yourself in the other person's shoes, you can often find solutions that mean everyone feels OK again. Understanding each other's feelings and points of view – even if we don't agree – is the key to dealing with conflict confidently.

For example, Pip's classmate Bop was tapping their pencil loudly while Pip was trying to concentrate. Pip could show feelings of annoyance and tell Bop angrily to be quiet, or Pip could hide these feeling and ignore the tapping.

Pip thinks: to solve the problem, it's important to stand up for myself... but also to see if I can understand why Bop is tapping the pencil!

Pip could say: "Hey, that noise is putting me off – can you stop? Are you having trouble with this question? It's a tough one."

This way both Pip's and Bop's feelings are respected.

How could you resolve these arguments and conflicts fairly, so everyone's feelings are important and you both feel OK?

1   You and your brother both want to play on the computer – he says it's his turn, you say it's yours. What will you do?

_____

_____

2   Your friend's favourite game has gone missing. They say you hid it when you visited their house. What will you do?

_____

_____

3   You and your friend turn up to a party wearing the same top. You think your friend is copying you. What will you do?

_____

_____

♥ **Feeling OK when there's conflict is a big part of growing confidence – that way, we know that even if things don't go according to plan, they'll still work out alright.**

ACTIVITY: I'M A SECRET SUPERHERO!

Imagine you had a secret life as a super-confident superhero. What would you do with the power of confidence? Can you write or draw a story about how you'd use your powers? What would happen if your superhero self had the same challenges you do in your real life?

Think of three problems, challenges or things you find hard at the moment. Then imagine what superhero-you would do in these situations…

Challenge 1

Challenge 2

Challenge 3

I CAN DO
HARD THINGS

Find your voice

Your ideas, opinions and feelings are important. You are special because you are you, and what you have to say is welcome in the world!

It can feel scary to speak up – answering questions in class, disagreeing with a friend or asking for help – and it sometimes feels easier to keep quiet. But if you don't speak up, those around you will never get to hear your ideas or know what you need. They won't get to learn about how wonderful you are and they'll miss out on sharing the brilliant, interesting things that are in your unique mind.

Practise speaking with a clear, confident voice in front of the mirror! Try these phrases, or make up your own:

ACTIVITY: WHAT MAKES ME SHINE?

When do you feel really good and really confident? That's when you shine brightest! It might be when you're doing something you have practised a lot, with someone special to you, doing something creative or in a place where you feel amazing.

Pip shines brightest when there's music, dancing and friends around!

Can you write about the people, places and activities that make you shine?

The people who make me shine are…

_____

_____

_____

The places I shine brightest are…

I shine brightly when I…

CONFIDENCE IS MY SUPERPOWER

ACTIVITY: MAKE AN INNER STRENGTH BADGE

What are the things about you that make you strong? Maybe it's your kindness, determination or your big heart. It can be difficult to come up with answers to this question, so why not ask your parent or carer for ideas if you get stuck.

Write your strengths on the badges on the next page, and decorate them however you like!

When you've finished, cut out your badges and add a safety pin so you can wear them, or stick them up in your room to remind you how strong and wonderful you are.

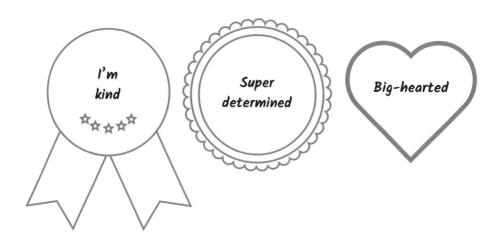

Be careful when cutting out this page

MY BEST IS BEST FOR ME

Be your own best friend

Do you have a best friend? Some people do, some don't. Have a go at thinking about the things that make a wonderful best friend for you. You can write them down here:

_____

_____

_____

_____

_____

_____

Now, can you imagine being all of those things for yourself? It might sound strange but it works! Think about it: we're always with ourselves, and our thoughts mean we're always sort of talking to ourselves.

Everyone's list will be slightly different, but yours might look a little like the list on page 65 of what makes a true friend.

When you act like a best friend to yourself, you build confidence from within. Speaking to yourself kindly, treating your ideas and your body with respect, doing things you enjoy… It's like having a little confidence coach with you all the time!

ACTIVITY: AFFIRMATIONS

Affirmations are short sentences that work like magic on your self-confidence. Saying them every day is like casting a spell on yourself. Even if the words don't feel true yet, your mind will start to believe them a little more each day.

Give these a go and see how saying them makes you feel. Why not write them on coloured paper and stick them somewhere you'll see every day?

ACTIVITY: HOW YOU THINK AFFECTS YOUR CONFIDENCE

Did you know that thoughts are very powerful things? The way we think about ourselves and the world determines a lot of the emotions we feel and the choices we make.

Being unkind to yourself and believing the world is an unkind place for you to live in are examples of negative thoughts. There's nothing wrong with thinking negative thoughts – everyone does some of the time.

Do you ever find yourself getting stuck in negative thoughts? They can be a real confidence shrinker! Next time you feel like your thoughts are getting you down, write them here:

_____

_____

_____

_____

_____

_____

_____

Now, what would you say to your best friend if they thought these things about themselves? Can you answer your negative thoughts with kinder, more positive ones?

_____

_____

_____

_____

_____

_____

_____

What if I don't win?

A lot of the time, when it comes to sport, exams or competitions – the kind of things that need the most confidence – we think about winners and losers. Perhaps we even think if we're not perfect or not the best, we lose.

There's another way to think about winning that might help build your confidence. What if you weren't competing against other people…? What if you're always just competing against fear? So, if something is scary or new and you need bravery to try it, the only way you can lose is by not trying it. You might come last in a race, or you might come first in it – either way, you beat fear by feeling scared and doing it anyway. You win!

ACTIVITY: I AM BRILLIANT!

We're all good at different things. What are your skills? Perhaps you're a good cook, great at telling jokes or you're proud of the way you draw. Celebrate your skills by writing them down here:

_____

_____

_____

Now write down something you'd like to improve:

_____

_____

_____

What could you do to get better at this?

_____

_____

_____

Can you think of something you can't do **yet**... but would like to try?

_____

_____

_____

_____

_____

_____

How could you learn to do that?

_____

_____

_____

_____

_____

_____

ACTIVITY: EVERYONE WAS ONCE A BEGINNER

It's easy to look at others – sportspeople, singers, musicians, famous authors, YouTubers… even other kids at school – and think that they're naturally good at the things they're good at. The truth is, we don't get to see the hard work and practice that people put into building the skills and confidence that they can later impress us with.

So, if you ever feel silly or annoying asking for help or for needing time to learn, try to remember that everyone – yes, even your favourite celebrity – was once a beginner.

To help you remember this, fill in the blanks with people you admire – they could be famous or people you know, kids or adults.

_____ *was once a beginner at* _____.

On their first tries, _____ *wasn't an expert at* _____.

When they first started out, _____ *couldn't* _____ *very well.*

_____ *made mistakes while learning how to* _____.

ACTIVITY: WORKING TOGETHER

Three friends are going camping together – Amy, Connor and Keisha. They're very different, but they're the best of friends.

Amy is good at making plans, but finds change very hard. She finds a really great spot to set up camp, and makes sure the gang have fun things to do every day.

Connor is very creative, but finds it difficult to concentrate on one thing at a time. When it rains unexpectedly, he works out a clever way to keep everything dry, and invents a game they can play inside the tent.

Keisha is really brave, but she can be impatient. Out walking by herself, she finds an amazing climbing tree and runs back to show the others.

Between them they have so many strengths! If they were all the same type of person, the camping trip might not have been so much fun.

Instead of comparing their strengths and weaknesses, the three friends work together and let each other be themselves.

In what ways are you different from your closest friends? Can you name your strengths and weaknesses?

_____

_____

_____

_____

_____

_____

_____

I AM
ENOUGH

PART 4: LOOKING AFTER YOURSELF

Looking after yourself means making sure you get enough sleep, eat enough healthy food, move your body enough and let your feelings show – the nice ones and the trickier ones. It's the job of the grown-ups who look after you to help with this, but you are a big part of it too! It's a good idea to learn the reasons why looking after your whole self is important.

When your body is well taken care of, it's easier to do something called "emotional regulation".

Emotional regulation

Emotional regulation means when you feel a big emotion, you're able to stay in control and bring yourself back to a calm feeling.

It's something that's hard for children, and it gets easier as you get older. You can ask for help – even grown-ups need help with this sometimes! There's no rush and it's very normal for kids your age to find it difficult to calm down after feeling something big – whether it's a nice emotion like excitement, or a hard one like sadness.

Feeling calm is a big part of feeling confident. When you're about to do something brave, big emotions like fear can bubble up in your body. When you're tired, hungry or full of energy or emotions, it's harder to calm those big feelings and do brave things. The activities in this chapter will help you learn about taking care of your whole self.

ACTIVITY: DESIGN A SMOOTHIE

Eating lots of colourful fruits and vegetables will ensure you get all the vitamins and minerals your body needs to feel at its best.

Drinking a smoothie is one really great way of getting a mix of fruits and vegetables into your body, and they're easy to make!

What would go in your ideal smoothie? You can choose from this page, or add your own!

Pick your fruit

Pick your vegetables

Add some extras

♥ **Why not ask a grown-up to help you try out your recipe?**

ACTIVITY: SWEET DREAMS

After a good night's sleep you'll wake up feeling ready for anything! If you have trouble dropping off at night, try jotting down your thoughts in a sleep diary before you go to sleep and when you wake up in the morning.

Before you go to sleep, you could ask yourself:

How tired do I feel?
What's on my mind?
Is any part of me uncomfortable?

When you wake up, you can ask:

Did I have any dreams?
What helped me fall asleep?
How am I feeling?

♥ Writing down your thoughts like this clears your mind, which will mean you fall asleep more easily, as well as helping you keep track of your sleeping habits.

ACTIVITY: GET PLENTY OF EXERCISE

Being active is super important for keeping your body healthy, but did you know it keeps your brain healthy too? Exercising and moving your body releases special feel-good chemicals in your brain, helping you feel happier and more confident. Can you draw yourself doing your favourite kind of exercise? (It doesn't need to be a sport – dancing, running around with your friends and climbing trees are all excellent exercise too!)

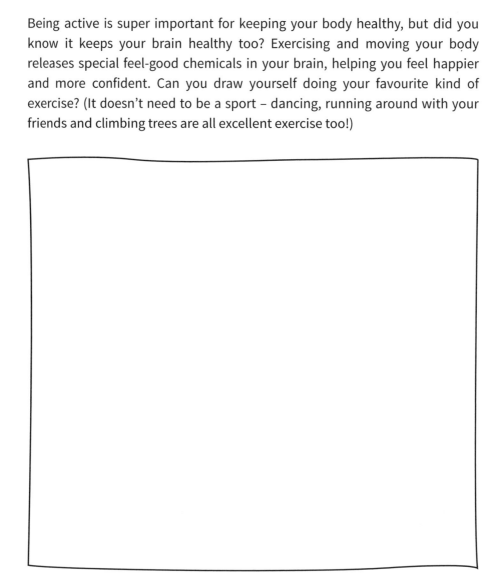

ACTIVITY: PLAYING IS IMPORTANT!

Your brain is growing every day, and one of the most powerful ways of helping it grow is by playing. Play isn't just for little kids… The way we play just changes as we get older.

How do you like to play?

Drawing, construction toys, colouring, exploring outdoors, writing stories or poems, art, reading, collecting… Whatever activities you love to get lost in are play!

Can you write or draw about your absolute favourite type of play?

ACTIVITY: EATING HEALTHILY

What are your favourite foods? Do you wish you could eat them every day, for every meal? Your body needs lots of different foods to grow strong and healthy, so having your favourites three times a day would make you feel tired and possibly make you ill!

To feel your best and be your strongest, you need a whole rainbow of foods. Can you draw different foods for each of the colours of the rainbow?

Time to relax

When you relax, you can breathe deeply and think clearly, making you naturally more confident. But it can sometimes be tricky to slow down your mind and relax your body. Try this technique next time you're having trouble relaxing.

Picture a place where you feel safe – it could be a real place you know, or an imaginary place. Spend some time putting lots of detail into this place. Make sure there are a lot of soothing things around. Use all your senses – what does your place smell like? What can you hear? How does the ground feel under your feet? If there's food there, what does it taste like?

You can go to this place in your mind any time, changing or adding details, or just being there and feeling calm.

I DESERVE
TO SHINE

ACTIVITY: KEEP SAFE ON THE INTERNET

The internet can be a great place – there's so much information and fun out there! But it's important to keep safe when you're online. If you can remember a few simple rules, you'll be able to make the most of the internet with confidence.

Can you design a poster to help you and your family remember this? You could choose one or more rule to focus on.

- Never post your personal information or passwords online

- Never befriend someone you don't know

- Never meet up with someone you've met online

- Think carefully before you post pictures or words on the internet

- If you see something online that makes you feel uncomfortable, unsafe or worried, leave the website, turn off your computer and tell a trusted adult immediately

Draw your poster design here:

I AM
SPECIAL

A balanced life

It's OK to want different things at different times – you're a unique, growing human being, and your needs change all the time. Sometimes Pip wants to be silly with friends; other times Pip wants to read quietly alone… and that's OK!

All human beings need a mix of the following things in their lives:

- ♥ Rest

- ♥ Exercise

- ♥ Time to concentrate

- ♥ Time to think

- ♥ Relaxation

- ♥ Play

- ♥ Connection with others

So, listen to your body and remember that you can ask for what you need, and that what you need is allowed to change.

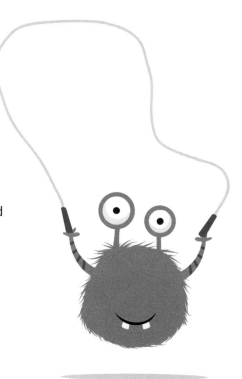

ACTIVITY: MAKE A CONFIDENCE BOX

When we need help to feel calm and confident, there are certain things that can help us. These will be different for everyone – they might include pictures, a squeezy toy, a piece of soft fabric, a lucky stone, a favourite quote, a journal for writing down thoughts… whatever works for you. Why not decorate a shoebox and keep the objects that help you feel relaxed and confident in there? That way, they're all in one place whenever you need them.

What kind of thing would go in your confidence box? Write a list before you start gathering objects to go in there.

♥ _____

♥ _____

♥ _____

♥ _____

♥ _____

♥ _____

♥ _____

♥ _____

♥ _____

I CAN
DO IT!

PART 5: FACING YOUR FEARS

What have you learned so far in this book? Perhaps that some of the ideas and confidence boosters are helpful for you, and others less so – and that's OK! A big part of confidence comes from trusting yourself and knowing what's right for you.

When you trust yourself, you find the bravery to face your fears – big ones and small ones. Being brave looks different for everyone and changes all the time. All sorts of things can be scary for all sorts of people.

This chapter is about the confidence that comes from finding the bravery to do what's scary to *you*.

ACTIVITY: NAME YOUR FEARS

What is scary to you? Use this space to jot down all the things – big and small – that make you feel scared, anxious or worried.

_____

_____

_____

_____

_____

_____

_____

_____

_____

ACTIVITY: DRAW YOURSELF AS A WARRIOR

Can you draw yourself as a fearless warrior on the next page? You might like to add armour or special accessories, like Pip! What would your battle cry be?

Draw yourself as a warrior here:

- ♥ Would you have armour and special powers? Would you pull a particular pose? How would your face look? Would you have a warrior name or your own name?

I AM
BRAVE

ACTIVITY: I WAS BRAVE WHEN...

Can you think of a time you overcame a challenge? It might seem like a big or a small challenge to others, but every time you act with bravery it's a big deal. Maybe you felt scared or worried about going to a party but went anyway, or you stood up for yourself or your friends against someone being mean? Write or draw about one or more times you've been strong and brave in the past, including as much detail as possible:

What was the problem or challenge?

How did you act with bravery?

What happened in the end?

ACTIVITY: GROW CONFIDENCE, SHRINK FEAR

Can you imagine what fear looks like? How about confidence? Can you draw the two emotions here?

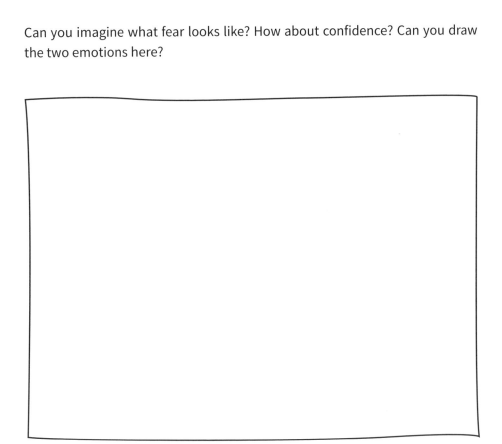

Now picture yourself shrinking fear with the power of your confidence – as the fear gets smaller, your confidence gets bigger.

The truth is, the emotion of fear or anxiety will never completely go away – after all, it's a normal, healthy feeling that we all experience – but you can choose how much you listen to it. Often, it helps to talk about feelings with someone you trust. Simply saying "I feel scared/worried/sad" can help shrink that feeling a little bit.

Surprise yourself

If you're used to not doing things because you feel scared, acting with confidence is going to feel extra difficult for you.

You're doing brilliantly and it's OK to take things slowly.

Start by doing one small thing that scares you. That might be talking about your feelings, trying something new or asking for help.

See what happens when you make a brave choice – you might surprise yourself!

What small brave thing could you do to surprise yourself?

_____

_____

_____

_____

_____

_____

I AM POWERFUL!

ACTIVITY: VISUALIZE A MORE CONFIDENT YOU

Think back to the superhero activity on page 70, when you imagined what you'd do with the superpower of confidence. Can you imagine yourself with that superpower again? This time, close your eyes and see yourself as you are right now but more confident. You don't have to do anything – just feel the feeling of confidence and see yourself feeling it in your mind.

Make a note of what's different about yourself when you think of a more confident you, and what's the same. You could draw, doodle, brainstorm, write a poem… whatever feels right!

I AM LEARNING AND GROWING EVERY DAY

ACTIVITY: ALL EMOTIONS ARE OK

However you feel, your emotions are OK – you are allowed to feel the way you feel. If something is too much and you can't find the bravery for it today, be kind to yourself – you can try again another time when you're feeling stronger.

What counts is what we do with our feelings. It's worth getting to know how different emotions affect us, and what helps us when experiencing big or tricky emotions.

Can you complete the following sentences?

When I feel angry I _____.

When I'm angry it feels good to _____.

When I'm scared I _____.

When I'm scared it feels good to _____.

When I'm sad I _____.

When I'm sad it feels good to _____.

PART 6: A CONFIDENT FUTURE

Hopefully you've learned a lot about yourself and about confidence by reading this book. Acting with confidence is a habit rather than something about you that needs fixing or can be changed quickly. What takes confidence will change as you get older – a lot of the things you find difficult now will become easier, some things you find easy now might start to feel difficult, and there are loads of new experiences you'll have, some of which will require bravery.

In this chapter we'll think about how you can keep your confidence growing in the future.

ACTIVITY: BRAVERY JAR

Every time you act with strength, bravery and confidence is a cause for celebration. Make sure you remember all your moments of bravery by writing them down and keeping them together in a special jar.

Why not decorate your jar with a crown? Use the one on the page opposite as a template to design your own, then cut it out and wrap it around your jar, using sticky tape to keep it in place.

Keeping your accomplishments together like this means the next time you need a boost of confidence, you can take a look back at all the amazing things you've achieved.

Celebrate yourself

It can feel uncomfortable sometimes to act with confidence and speak about your achievements. You might be worried that your friends will like you less if you start standing up for yourself, disagreeing with them sometimes or acting with bravery that they don't yet have.

Jealousy is a hard emotion to feel, and many people feel jealous of confident, brave people. So, be kind to others, but do not stick around if they try to bring you down. Remember: if another person is unkind to you because you stand up for yourself or tell the truth about your feelings, that's not your fault. Other people can feel hard emotions just like you can, and it's not your job to try to stop them feeling those emotions.

Celebrate yourself and value yourself enough to speak up when something isn't right. It's not easy and takes a lot of bravery, but you can do it! What's more, you will inspire others to act with bravery too.

ACTIVITY: WORDS TO REMEMBER

What words make you feel strong, confident and powerful? You might have found some good ones in this book or you might have a favourite quote… or you might make up your own!

Write the words that give you a boost in these spaces, then cut them out (be careful with the scissors) and stick them where you'll see them every day.

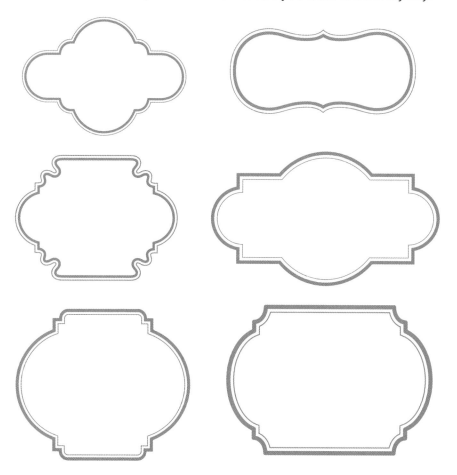

Be careful when cutting out this page

ACTIVITY: VISUALIZE YOUR DAY

Try drawing or writing about how you'd like your day (or week/month/year) to go. Take a little time in the morning to picture yourself acting with confidence and things going your way.

Give it a try in the space below. How would you like your day to turn out?

_____

_____

_____

_____

_____

ACTIVITY: CONFIDENCE ACTION PLAN

What tools help you feel more confident? We put some objects together in a confidence box on page 109, but now let's make a plan of action.

Here are some ideas from the book to get you started:

- ♥ Take a break

- ♥ Do some breathing exercises (pages 49–50)

- ♥ Go to my safe place (page 103)

- ♥ Move my body

- ♥ Write it down

- ♥ Talk to _____

- ♥ Use visualization (page 123)

When I feel low in confidence, I can...

The end

Pip feels a lot more confident now – do you too?

You can come back to this book any time to remind yourself of how confidence and bravery work, of your confidence boosters and shrinkers, or to look back on the activities you completed.

You've done incredibly well to work through this book – it's certainly not easy.

Goodbye and good luck.

Always remember: you are strong, brave and confident!

I AM CONFIDENT!

For parents: what you can do to help boost your child's confidence

Boosting your child's confidence is a tricky thing. It requires a balance between allowing them their independence and offering supportive encouragement. You know your child better than anyone and you can trust yourself to get that balance right. Even if you feel you've made a mistake, you can learn from it and choose differently next time.

One of the greatest gifts you can give your child is simply to be there and listen. Let them know they are not alone and that their feelings are valid.

You can also work to set a good example of feeling unsure but doing it anyway – that's bravery and confidence at any age. Vocalize your thought processes when there's a problem – try using positive, solutions-based language. Tell them about something you used to find difficult but now feels easier. Talk about your feelings, what you still find difficult and how you find bravery. This way your child will understand that everyone is different, imperfect and brave in their own way.

It can be tempting to try to inflate your child's confidence with lots of praise – but be wary of this as they get wise to it very quickly! Instead, try to be specific with your praise – focus on small improvements and the things you know are hard for them. Compliment their bravery and tell them how much you love them. Even when they have seemingly taken a step back, let them know you see that they are trying their best and are proud of them.

Peer pressure can start to ramp up at this age, and it takes huge strength to be yourself in the face of it. So, let your child know that you value their uniqueness, that it's OK to feel different and it's OK to find things hard. Try to encourage them gently toward positive and diverse role models, and feed their imagination with inspiring books, films and activities.

I hope this book has been helpful for you and your child. It's always hard to see your child shrinking back or missing out on life due to a lack of confidence, and you're doing a fantastic job by helping and supporting them in working through their feelings. On the next few pages you'll find suggestions for further reading and advice, so I will leave you here and wish you all the very best of luck!

Further advice

If you're worried about your child's mental health, do talk it through with your GP. While almost all children experience feelings of low confidence, some may need extra help. There are loads of great resources out there for information and guidance on children's mental health:

Mind
www.mind.org.uk
0300 123 3393
info@mind.org.uk
Text: 86463

BBC Bitesize
www.bbc.co.uk/bitesize/support

Childline
www.childline.org.uk
0800 1111

Recommended reading

You Are Awesome: Find Your Confidence and Dare to Be Brilliant at (Almost) Anything by Matthew Syed
Wren & Rook, 2018

Banish Your Self-Esteem Thief: A Cognitive Behavioural Therapy Workbook on Building Positive Self-Esteem for Young People
Kate Collins-Donnelly
Jessica Kingsley Publishers, 2014

Stand Up for Yourself & Your Friends: Dealing with Bullies & Bossiness and Finding a Better Way
Patti Kelley Criswell
American Girl Publishing, 2016

The Story Cure: An A–Z of Books to Keep Kids Happy, Healthy and Wise
Ella Berthoud and Susan Elderkin
Canongate, 2017

Image credits

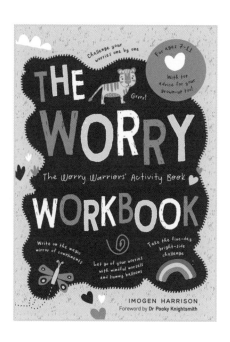

THE WORRY WORKBOOK

The Worry Warriors' Activity Book

Imogen Harrison

£10.99

Paperback

ISBN: 978-1-78783-537-5

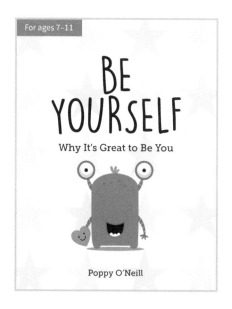

BE YOURSELF

Why It's Great to Be You

Poppy O'Neill

£10.99

Paperback

ISBN: 978-1-78783-608-2

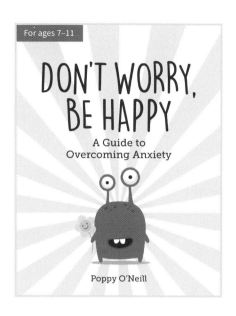

DON'T WORRY, BE HAPPY

A Guide to
Overcoming Anxiety

Poppy O'Neill

£10.99

Paperback

ISBN: 978-1-78685-236-6

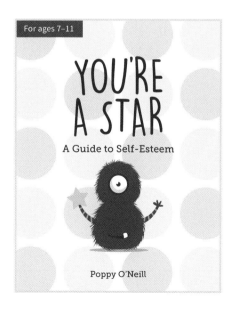

YOU'RE A STAR

A Guide to Self-Esteem

Poppy O'Neill

£10.99

Paperback

ISBN: 978-1-78685-235-9

Have you enjoyed this book?

If so, why not write a review on your favourite website?
If you're interested in finding out more about our books,
find us on Facebook at **Summersdale Publishers**
and follow us on Twitter at **@Summersdale**.

Thanks very much for buying this Summersdale book.

www.summersdale.com